Justin's Jumper

Written by Narinder Dhami
Illustrated by Jen Khatun

Collins

Gran had stopped by to see Justin.

"I have a present for you," Gran said. She handed Justin a gift box.

He grinned and lifted the lid.

Gran's gift was a red jumper with big black spots …

"Thanks, Gran!" Justin gulped.

"I am glad you like it," Gran said, looking thrilled.

Justin slipped the jumper on. It hung like a tent!

"Dad, this jumper is rubbish!" he moaned.

"Justin!" Dad snapped. "Gran spent weeks finishing it for you!"

Justin felt bad. But he was meeting Brad and Fliss at the park. He was NOT keen on them seeing the jumper!

The twins were waiting near the park.
"Is that a jumper?" said Fliss.
"Or a dress?" said Brad.

Justin and the twins swung on the swings until they needed a drink.

The benches were full, so Justin and Fliss sat on the jumper.

"It's soft, like a blanket!" said Fliss.

Brad did a handstand, but he kept wobbling. So Justin strapped Brad to the bench with his jumper!

"Thanks, Justin!" Brad yelled.

Then Justin spotted a dog running off.
He trapped it with his jumper and grabbed it.

Frank and Blossom were in the park too.
Blossom was wailing.

"She lost her balloon," sighed Frank.
"Now she will not stop howling!"

Justin laid the jumper on Blossom's lap. She grinned.

"You are a champ, Justin!" said Frank.

Justin was fond of his jumper now.
It had helped a lot today.

Frank was right. It was a jumper fit for a champ!

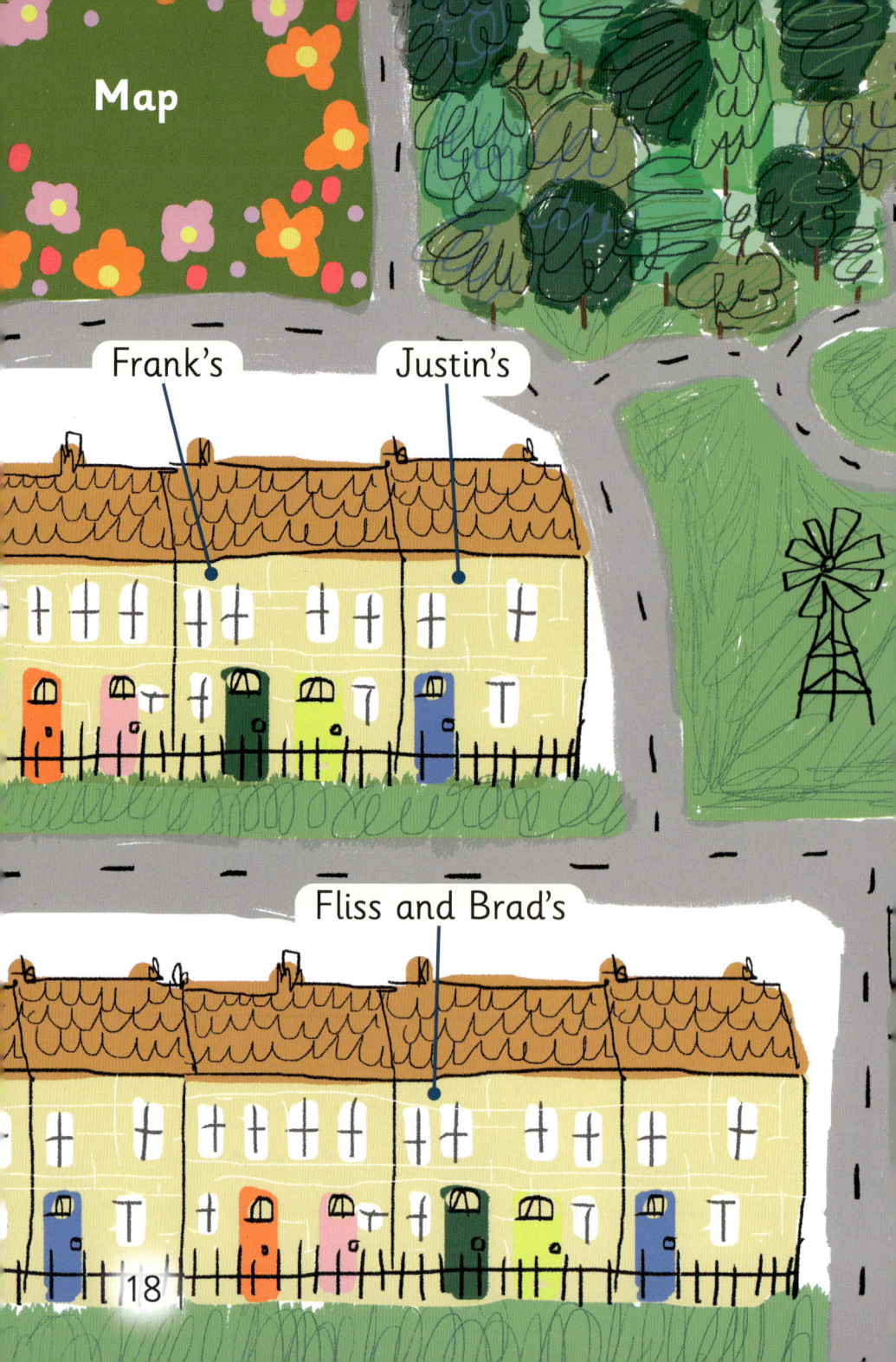

Biggest jumper

A jumper smashed the record for the biggest jumper ever! It's 18.5 m long. That's as long as a big truck!

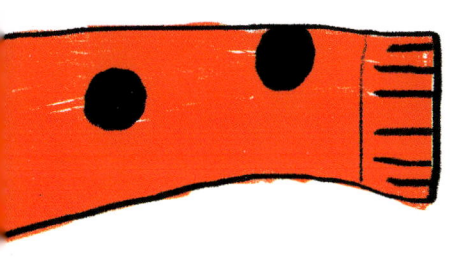
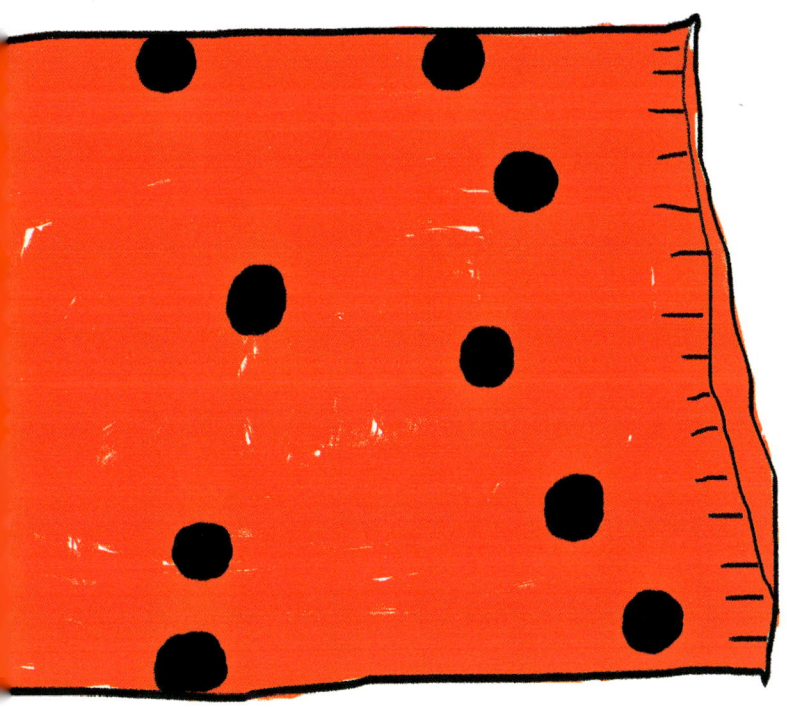

How did Justin's jumper help?

extra bench

handstand strap

dog trapper

howl stopper

Review: After reading

Use your assessment from hearing the children read to choose any words or tricky words that need additional practice.

Read 1: Decoding
- Ask the children to read page 6. Say: Can you sound out the words in your head silently, before reading them aloud? Focus on the meaning of **rubbish** and **snapped** in context. Ask:
  o What does **rubbish** mean here? (e.g. *very bad, unwearable*)
  o What does **snapped** tell you about the way Dad spoke? (e.g. *he spoke sharply, angrily – like a bite*)
- Encourage the children to read these words by sounding out each letter and blending.

spent	**twins**	**present**	**blanket**
bench	**gift**	**handstand**	

- Bonus content: Challenge the children to read page 20 fluently. Discuss the meaning of **smashed** in context. Ask: What does it mean here? (*beat, broke*) Discuss how this is different in other contexts, such as a smashed vase.

Read 2: Prosody
- Turn to pages 4 and 5. Read each sentence, focusing on the punctuation. Ask:
  o What should we do when we see an ellipsis? (*pause*) Why pause here? (e.g. *to create suspense, we have to wait and see what happens next*)
  o The exclamation mark means we need to read with extra feeling – how is Justin feeling? (e.g. *shocked, surprised*)
  o Discuss the commas and how they break up the sentences.
- Encourage the children to read both pages aloud, using the punctuation to guide their pauses and expression.

Read 3: Comprehension
- Ask the children if they have something that they are fond of (or dislike) wearing. Ask: Why do you like (or not like) it so much?
- Turn to pages 14 and 15. Ask: Why was Blossom wailing? (*she had lost her balloon*) Why did she stop crying? (e.g. *Justin's jumper comforted her*)
- Ask the children to explain how and why Justin felt differently about his new jumper. Use pages 22 and 23 as prompts to help the children recall each event.